Pregnant with Purpose

Purpose:[1]

That which a person sets before himself as an object to be reached or accomplished; the end or aim to which the view is directed in any plan, measure or exertion. We believe the Supreme Being created intelligent beings for some benevolent and glorious Purpose, and if so, how glorious and benevolent must be His Purpose in the Plan of Redemption!

---

[1] http://av1611.com/kjbp/kjv-dictionary/purpose.html

Dedication

I wish to present this book to all women across the globe pregnant with Dreams, Visions, Purpose and Destiny.

Thank you for your support!

PREGNANT WITH PURPOSE

MAH- TOSHA NANCE

Pregnant with Purpose

Scripture quotations are taken from the following Bibles:

(NIV) are taken from the Holy Bible, New International Version®, NIV®. Copyright © 1973, 1978, 1984, 2011 by Biblica, Inc. ™ Used by permission of Zondervan. All rights reserved worldwide. www.zondervan.com The "NIV" and "New International Version" are trademarks registered in the United States Patent and Trademark Office by Biblica, Inc.™

ESV® Bible (The Holy Bible, English Standard Version®), copyright © 2001 by Crossway, a publishing ministry of Good News Publishers. Used by permission. All rights reserved.

The New King James Version (NKJV) ®. Copyright © 1982 by Thomas Nelson. Used by permission. All rights reserved.

Copyright © 2017 by Mah-Tosha Nance

Cover created by: Yrvens J. of YJDesigns - hello@yjdesigns.co

Interior Design: Beverly E. Barracks - bebarracks@gmail.com

Printed by: Printed by CreateSpace, An Amazon.com Company @ www.createspace.com

All Rights Reserved. This book or any portion thereof may not be reproduced or used in any form or any manner whatsoever without the express written permission of the author except for the use of brief quotations in a book review. Please direct all inquiries to pregnantwithpurposebook@gmail.com.

ISBN-13: 978-0692050873
ISBN-10: 0692050876

Printed in the United States of America

Foreword

Perhaps you may be a member of the critical mass that question why do I exist or those that ask the question for what reason was I born? Maybe you've struggled to find the answer to the question – why do I seem to be so different than everyone else? Why does my reality and beliefs take me into places and spaces that makes it hard for others to understand me? Why do I seem to be stuck and not progressing even though I am a beautiful, intelligent, and well-equipped person? If this is you, I believe your steps and timing have been divinely ordered to hold this book in your hands and prepared to consume the vast content and principles contained in it.

If discovering the answers to assist you in discovery of your purpose or to clarify steps you need to take in order to fulfill your purpose is what you are seeking, I don't believe you need to look any further. Your answers, motivation and inspiration are right here – everything you need to know to wake up purpose and make it work for you and the people you attract. The tools, techniques, and technology to overcome stagnation and begin to accelerate into an ascended place and position are being held in your hands at this very moment. Somewhere in the depths of your consciousness, an important place in your mind, you have desired to attain the information presented in this book or you would not have found yourself in possession of it.

Some might say *"you can't beat God's timing"!* Sometimes our lives seemingly tend to be calculated and orchestrated in ways that appear to be both strange and weird. We haven't quite known why we have made the choices we made. We

Foreword

don't understand how we ended up where we are right now. We can't always account for the people that have been on this journey with us. However, what we must do is understand that the path we are on to accomplish the purpose of the journey is not a mistake. The path of the journey called life has many curves, ebb tides and flows, as well as twists and turns that will not all make sense to you in the current moment of the experience.

But, when you authentically begin to seek the empowering answers, you will have a collision with some of the most amazing people in the world to assist you by bringing light onto your path. For you, the individual ready to devour the contents of this high-powered testimony of purpose, one such person is Ms. Mah-Tosha Nance. As an author and genuine spiritual being, she has composed the thoughts of her mind and heart in such a way that it will clearly point you in the right direction to explore your own purpose and significance within this life. You've asked for it, and now you have it!

With no hesitation, I know that you will be impressed, inspired and absolutely blessed by what you find in the midst of the forthcoming pages. I know that reading this book will either cause you to conceive or acknowledge that you are indeed Pregnant with Purpose yourself. In other words, carefully consuming the contents found here is almost assured to produce a turning point in your life. Here is not only a testimony of a young girl defying the odds of her experience and blossoming into a beautiful butterfly, but an easy to read and understand explanation of how to give birth to your purpose. The author will inspire and motivate you to conquer any limitations or setbacks you've experienced leaving no room for excuse rather than expectancy.

I encourage you to invest the time in reading every word found here and do everything the author suggests. Undoubtedly, you will find that it will answer all the questions you have diligently asked within the confines of your heart and mind. Pay attention to this material so that your purpose will manifest; thus, transforming your mind and life.

David D. Bynes, M.Ed.
The OutPour Freedom Center, Sr. Apostolic Leader/Founder
Destiny Speaks Coaching & Consulting, CEO/Founder
Fort Lauderdale, Florida

Contents

Dedication iv

Foreword v

Introduction 1

Chapter One: "WOW! I AM Pregnant" 5

Chapter Two: "Identify When You Conceived" 11

Chapter Three: "Avoid The Desire To Abort" 17

Chapter Four: "Do Not Lose It" 21

Chapter Five: "Don't Get Stuck In The Tube" 29

Chapter Six: "Don't Put Me In A Box" 33

Chapter Seven: "Identify What You Are Carrying" 37

Chapter Eight: "Rejection Will Not Stop Me" 45

Chapter Nine: "Move Past Intimidation" 49

Chapter Ten: "Don't Be Distracted By The Noise" 51

Chapter Eleven: "Do Not Move Before Time" 59

Chapter Twelve: "Release the Hurt" 63

Chapter Thirteen: "It's Time To Deliver" 69

Prayer 71

Introduction

*O*nce your spirit man gets connected with the Creator; the Trinity: the Father, the Son and the Holy Spirit, God's DNA will begin to flutter within your 'womb' (even if you are male); giving you an awareness that there is life within, though small.

Suddenly, revelation takes place and all the hardships, setbacks, curve balls and difficulties I experienced in life thus far, was to bring me to this place in time. Yet, I felt stuck in a continuous cycle of going between school, work, church, and home. I knew that I was placed here on earth for more, there had to be more; but I was stuck, I felt cemented in place.

I was inspired to write this book because I knew I was carrying Purpose, but nevertheless I was stuck. God kept speaking to me about what I should be doing, but I just couldn't seem to get out of the formation stage; I was stuck. My thoughts were, maybe I am not worthy,

Introduction

capable or smart enough. I was stuck associating myself with people who were comfortable where they were and my state of being, provided comfort to them; our lives mirrored each other. They refused to recognize that I was carrying something greater on the inside of me. They couldn't sense that I was pregnant with Purpose both *spiritually* and *naturally*; if they did, they refused to acknowledge it. Knowing and accepting that I was carrying Purpose caused my perspective to change. I made up in my mind that I had to press in, in order to press on!

I pressed on and moved forward, in the direction of Purpose! God has placed each one of us here on earth fully equipped with a Purpose and you too can move forward towards it just as I did.

You're probably asking yourself—"how can I move forward; how can I fulfill my Purpose?" I am glad you asked. The very fact that you decided to read this book is the first step in moving forward in Purpose. As you continue to read, ask the Holy Spirit to connect your spirit with His; to help you identify what you are carrying; which trimester you are currently in, and how to prepare for delivery, because the baby you are carrying, is PURPOSE! You are Pregnant with Purpose.

***Romans* 8:28** – *"And we know that for those who love God all things work together for good, for those who are called according to his purpose."*

Chapter One

"WOW! I AM Pregnant"

Reflecting over my adolescent years, that period of my life was tempestuous to say the least. My mom had her own issues and lost her life at the hands of another; I was twelve years old. During that time, my father was on drugs and in and out of prison - (dad has since been delivered and now plays a big and important role in my life).

Lacking the proper parental covering, my life as a young adult continued a downward spiral. I became pregnant at the age of 17 by a guy that was 17 years my senior. I hid my pregnancy for seven (7) months. Because my sisters' and I were raised by my grandparents, and granddaddy was a preacher; we lived very restricted lives. If the church doors were open, best believe we had to be there. Being that my grandparents were the head of the church, I knew my pregnancy would not be well received by them, therefore, I was afraid to tell them.

I decided to share the news of my pregnancy with a friend-girl at church. I told her that no one knew, not even my grandparents. One day after church service the phone rang and my grandmother answered it. To my grandmother's surprise, she received news that she was not prepared for. It was the young lady I had shared my secret with. She told my grandmother, *"your granddaughter Mah-Tosha is pregnant and you need to take her to the doctor."* When my grandmother hung up the phone and looked at me, my heart dropped and I knew my secret was out. Betrayal is what I felt, but I didn't have time to express it because my grandmother told me that I had one week to inform my grandfather of the soon to be addition to our family.

If you knew my grandfather, you would know the fear that I was experiencing at that moment. I was beyond scared because he always warned my sisters' and I about the guys in our neighborhood and not to get tied up with them.

The end of the week felt like it arrived within 2 days. I hoped with all hope, that my grandmother had forgotten what she said I had to do, so I went to bed. But as fate would have it, she didn't. She woke me as soon as my grandfather arrived home and finished eating his dinner. The walk from my bedroom to the living room seemed like *"The Green Mile"* though we lived in a very modest home. As I walked, I felt faint and weak and began to stutter as I started to speak. Somehow, I was able to steady my words and say, *"Granddaddy, I'm pregnant."* He immediately said, *"Mah-Tosha, what have I told you? You get the guy responsible over here tomorrow so I can talk to him."* That's not all he said, but that's the only part of his response I am permitted to share.

Although, I had survived the initial conversation; I was still very much afraid. If you knew my grandfather, you would know this, he didn't play. I called the guy and he came over to talk to my grandfather. I wasn't allowed in the room while he spoke with the guy, so I never knew what my grandfather told him. In my naïve perception of reality, I thought the father was going to marry me, but that was far from the case; that was just wishful thinking.

I thought for sure my life was over; I was pregnant and so far behind in high school that it just made sense to dropout. My life at the time was headed in the wrong direction.

A turning point came later in my pregnancy, when I attended a family reunion. While there, family members repeatedly shared their memories of my mother's pregnancy with me. Others told me that I was special and different. They went on to say, *"there is something unique about you."* Even though my family saw the uniqueness in me, I failed to see it in myself. Ironically, none of them had a clue that I was pregnant. To prevent the knowledge of my pregnancy from spreading throughout the family, I wore bigger clothes. My small stature allowed the clothing to conceal my secret. I believe strongly that God used my family members to inform me that He had far more than just a life developing on the inside of me.

Those with spiritual insight can identify that you are carrying something even when you try your best to cover it up. We look at ourselves and see the layers we pile on to disguise our mistakes, type of family we come from, or the lack of an education. None of that matters to God, He knew all about us before we were formed in our mother's womb. He set us apart and called us who we are before we entered the world.

Jeremiah 1:5 – *"Before you were formed in the womb I knew you before you were born I set you apart; I appointed you as a prophet to the nations."*

> *"God knows you; the real you. Not the you that you want the world to see. The real you is perfect for the purpose He has for you."*

Chapter Two

"Identify When You Conceived"

When a woman discovers she's pregnant, she begins to experience bodily changes. Obvious signs are a missed or delayed period, fatigue, nausea, craving bizarre foods, and swollen breasts. The symptoms a woman may experience can differ from pregnancy to pregnancy. She carries each baby slightly different. When an individual conceives Purpose, they begin to feel differently, speak differently, and perceive differently. Just like a natural pregnancy must be confirmed, so must a spiritual pregnancy. The pregnant person should seek counseling from one more knowledgeable, to explain the new feelings, visions, and cravings. What used to bring one pleasure is now intolerable. What

Identify When You Conceived

you crave is unusual because it's not what you would normally feed on.

Now, just as you wouldn't trust an uneducated individual with your medical needs, be just as cautious with whom you trust when you are Pregnant with Purpose. Medical doctors train an average of twelve long years to become a board certified medical practitioner in the U.S. That's why you can tell them your symptoms, they run a test or two, and provide a diagnosis based on the test results. So, be very careful with whom you seek counsel from after you've conceived or identified that you are Pregnant with Purpose. If the individual hasn't received the necessary education or passed the required test, there's a strong possibility that you could be misdiagnosed.

That brings to mind the story of Mary. The biblical recount of Jesus' conception includes Mary (a virgin), the Holy Spirit (the third person of the Godhead), and the Angel Gabriel. To summarize *Luke 1:26-38,* Gabriel was sent to inform Mary of her highly favored status with God (the Father). Because of this favored status, she was chosen to conceive and bring forth a child that shall be named Jesus. Within his announcement, Gabriel gave her pertinent information about Jesus.

> *"He will be great, and will be called the Son of the Highest, and the Lord God will give Him the throne of his Father David. He shall reign over the house of Jacob forever; and his kingdom there should be no end" (v. 32-33).*

After receiving this information Mary questioned the angel about how this was supposed to happen. Gabriel told her that she wasn't to concern herself with that; conception was the job of the Holy Spirit.

Just like Mary was favored, chosen, and informed; God chooses, favors, and informs us of His plan for our lives. At the appointed time of conception, Mary had little knowledge of what she was favored to bring forth. Upon being informed of the greatness she would carry, Mary felt unqualified. At the conception of purpose, often the individual feels ill equipped, unaware of how it will happen, but has confidence in the result. That's why Mary went on to question "How can this be? I am a virgin." Mary made the same mistake we make. She looked to herself as the source of bringing about the Will of God instead of correctly viewing herself as the vessel.

As the vessel, she already had what was needed, a womb; a place to carry Purpose. Your role in the conception of your Purpose is to be the womb. The Angel of the Lord affirms, and the Holy Spirit performs.

So, there I was 17, pregnant, uneducated, and without a job to support a baby. The view from the *natural eye,* labeled me a statistic. I now understand that I was chosen by God to be a womb for my natural child and Purpose. A womb's primary function is to be a place where formation and development take place. Contrary to statistics, I was producing!

After conception, I started to have dreams, visions, ideas, and goals, but during pregnancy, a woman tends to forget quickly so I wrote all my ideas and visions down even though I was not yet at the place to give birth. At times, I didn't understand what was developing within me, and thought I was not capable. However, the proclamation of a positive pregnancy test, the affirmation of my family (as mentioned in Chapter One), and the anticipation of what was developing within my womb; let me know that God was doing something. The something God did was choose me to bring about His Purpose.

Matthew 22:14 – *"For many are called, but a few are chosen."*

> *"Just like Mary, the mother of Jesus was Chosen; you are Chosen!"*

Chapter Three

"Avoid The Desire To Abort"

An unwanted and/or unplanned pregnancy usually carries with it the negative stigma of shame, disgrace, guilt, fear, or selfishness. The mothers' perspective might be: "I am too young, I am still in school, others will know I am sexually active, I can't support or care for a child, I'm not married, I have too many children already, how can I share a kid with someone, I don't plan on spending the rest of my life with or I don't want to be a mother." Oftentimes, these reasons result in a decision to abort.

I remember when my grandparents initially learned of my pregnancy, they had no clue just how pregnant I was. I hid my pregnancy for a very long time. But a few days after finding out,

I was hauled off to an abortion clinic. The saving grace for my child was that at seven months, I was too far into the pregnancy to have had a safe abortion. Before judging my grandparents too harshly remember, I was their grandchild and at that time both were more than 60 years of age. This meant they would be raising an infant in their mid-sixties. I was adding to their financial burden, at a time both were looking to retire. It also added the physical burden of making space for and interacting with a newborn. Most importantly, they feared the influence a teenage pregnancy would have on my younger sisters.

Despite the fear that my grandparents and I felt, I went on to carry my baby to full term. Regrettably, a few years later I became pregnant again, but this time my negative circumstances convinced me to have an abortion. I chose to end my pregnancy because I feared failure. I feared responsibility because just as my grandparents had predicted, the obligation of raising my first born had fallen on them; as a result, I still did not understand what motherhood involved and I feared the future. The easy way out was to terminate the cause of my fear; my pregnancy.

Fear did its job, it persuaded me to kill what grew inside of me. How has fear persuaded you? One of fear's purpose is to *steal, kill and destroy* your Purpose.

John 10:10 - *"The thief comes only to steal and kill and destroy; I have come that they may have life, and have it more abundantly."*

Do not let fear steal from you, instead, turn that fear into faith by standing on the Word of God because, *"you can do all things through Christ that strengthens you—see **Philippians 4:13."*** So, whether you are pregnant spiritually with purpose or in the natural, do not abort your seed; do not kill your dream; do not kill your vision; and do not kill your purpose.

Mary, the mother of Jesus, could have chosen to abort her purpose by asking God to select another. Becoming pregnant when she did was both inconvenient to her and condemnable by Jewish law. It was inconvenient because she was scheduled to marry Joseph, and because of the pregnancy, Joseph wanted to put her away (annul the marriage); and from the onset of her pregnancy she feared persecution. However, God made provisions for each extenuating circumstance for the vision and His word to come to pass. Beyond the shadow of a doubt, Mary knew that God was with her and you should too.

Matthew 1:23 - *"The virgin will conceive and give birth to a son, and they will call him Immanuel" (which means "God is with us").*

> *"Just like God was with Mary, He is with us every step of the way."*

Chapter Four

"Do Not Lose It"

Studies reveal that anywhere from 10-25% of all clinically recognized pregnancies will end in miscarriage.[2] The first weeks of pregnancy are the most crucial. There are several reasons a miscarriage can happen, these are a few of them: hormonal problems; infections or maternal health problems; a woman's life style (i.e. smoking; drug use; malnutrition; excessive caffeine, alcohol and exposure to radiation or toxic substances; maternal age or maternal trauma.) When a woman becomes pregnant (whether natural or spiritual), her lifestyle must change because a precious seed has been planted within. She must first educate herself on what she is carrying, i.e. read books, go to seminars, conferences

---

[2] http://americanpregnancy.org/pregnancy-complications/miscarriage/

and go to the Doctor! Get around other people that have already given birth to what you are carrying and can cover you with prayer or an encouraging word whenever necessary.

Joseph covered Mary before the Angel spoke to him. He had purposed in his heart to put Mary away quietly because she became pregnant before they *'knew'* each other. It was unlawful for a woman to be found pregnant before she was married; Mary could have been stoned to death. But, because she was Pregnant with Purpose, God already had a plan in place. The Angel had to speak to Joseph and include him in the plan and Purpose of God for the mother to be, of His Son Jesus.

Allow me for a moment to travel down the road of being Pregnant with Purpose. I discovered during this season of my walk, how critical it is to have the right people around you who are ordained, chosen, and divinely connected to cover you and speak Life into your Life; your Purpose and Destiny is at hand.

Suddenly, I found myself in transition in ministry, on my job, writing my first book and starting my organization; leaving one place to go to another. I was so desperate for spiritual guidance that I positioned myself under the leadership of a man and woman that I thought could and would cover me and help push me into my destiny both spiritually and naturally.

I was so excited and ready to go through the process of being Pregnant with Purpose that I confided in them and exposed myself and told them everything about me so they could help push me forward into my Destiny. Sadly, I realized that I was under the wrong covering and they were not the ones God preordained to watch over my soul, and who could or would cover and guide me, as I walked out my process towards my Purpose and Destiny.

If I can impart one thing into you whether you are male or female, *as men can also be pregnant with spiritual purpose,* it would be this…. the moment you discover that you are Pregnant with Purpose, **PLEASE** be very prayerful with whom you share your Pregnancy.

Be intentional in seeking the Lord's guidance for the path He has preordained for you, and the people who He has divinely connected to accompany you during each trimester of your Pregnancy in order to fulfill your Purpose. Because as in the natural, there are seed/dream killers among you, walking to-and-fro looking to sabotage and cause you to miscarry. Keep in mind, the seed you are carrying is very precious, valuable and costly, as God Himself divinely placed it within.

Needless to say, I was very upset and hurt because they were totally the opposite of where God was taking me and what I was carrying. Through that process, I almost aborted what I was carrying; it caused confusion and delusion; and my drive and the burning fire deep within was close to being quenched.

But, GOD!!!

SUDDENLY, one morning I woke up and said, *"I will not lose what I have."* I prayed and asked God to connect me to the right people, give me clarity in hearing, sight and discernment; and guide me to not move by my emotions. Take heed that everything that looks good doesn't mean it is good for you. Pray and ask God for His divine connections during this critical season in your life. I started getting connected to the right people. Even though God was covering me the entire time; He wanted me to learn a lesson.

Who else do you have covering you, praying for you, interceding for you, guiding and mentoring you, educating and speaking into you, for your destiny, in your business or for your purpose? For example, you want to get married, but can that person cover you for where you are going? Is that person properly equipped for your Purpose and Destiny? Is the marriage a safe place? Remember, because you are carrying Purpose, you can't connect with just anyone and expect them to be equipped to effectively cover you, it has to be the right person.

Seek God, and He will lead and guide you to the right people whom He has predestined to cover you. God will always cover His investment. As it was with Joseph and Mary, an Angel of the Lord appeared to Joseph in a dream, and in the dream, he told Joseph *"do not be afraid to take Mary as your wife because the child within her was conceived by the Holy Spirit."* After hearing the Angel, Joseph was able to cover Mary. If you allow the Holy Spirit to guide and lead you, your chances become greater that you will not miscarry or lose what you are carrying by having the wrong people cover you. Also, make sure you are covered by spiritual parents that God ordained.

Romans 9:11 - *"though they were not yet born and had done nothing either good or bad—in order that God's purpose of election might continue, not because of works but because of him who calls."*

> *"God chooses people according to His Own Purpose"*

Part I

1st

TRIMESTER

Chapter Five

"Don't Get Stuck In The Tube"

I read about someone that got pregnant twice and each time her baby was stuck in her tube. When a woman has an *ectopic pregnancy*,[3] the fertilized egg implants itself outside of the uterus. Ninety-Five (95%) Percent of the time, it occurs in the tube which is a tubal pregnancy. After the fertilized egg implants itself in the fallopian tube and begins to develop, it is very dangerous and must be surgically removed.

Sometimes we get stuck in the tube of life due to procrastination. Procrastination is a challenge we have all faced at one point or another. For as long as humans have been

---

[3] A pregnancy in which the fetus develops outside the uterus, typically in a Fallopian tube.

around, we have been struggling with procrastinating on issues that matter to us.

We delay and postpone what we should be doing, and months and even years go by and we are still at the same place; stuck. We get stuck in between our now and our future; however, while we can set goals for our future, we can also begin to take action right now. It's so easy to get side tracked and delayed when we lose our focus.

I remember when God was telling me to write the book and start a non-profit organization. I kept putting things off and not doing what I was supposed to do. I put off going back to school, educating myself about non-profits and writing my book. Suddenly one day, God showed me an example of a clock. He said, *"the clock is steadily ticking, it never goes backwards or stands still, it is always moving forward."* In other words, He was telling me to move forward because time is steadily moving and will not wait for anyone. Being in the Will of God, you know that His direction is always to move Forward.

Mary didn't procrastinate or wait a couple of weeks or months to go visit her cousin

Elizabeth. She moved in God's divine timing immediately after the Angel had spoken with her. When she arrived and greeted Elizabeth, something *supernatural* happened to Elizabeth, the baby she had been carrying for six months without any movement whatsoever leaped, and Elizabeth was filled with joy and they were engulfed by the Glory of God. She told Mary that God had blessed her above all women and the child is blessed. I am honored that the mother of my Lord should visit me.

This was also confirmation for Mary. Most of the time when God speaks, He brings confirmation. If Mary would have procrastinated or waited to visit Elizabeth, she would have missed out on her confirmation. What are you missing, when you let procrastination slip in?

Sometimes when we put things off or on hold, we put God's timing off for our lives and the plans and purpose He has for us. One day of delay can suddenly turn into one month, and before you know it, it will be two months, and a new year of wasted time. When we procrastinate, we also forfeit our divine connections strategically positioned along the path of our life's journey.

It's time to purpose in your heart and make up your mind to no longer allow procrastination to get in your way of writing that book, starting that business, begin your career or go back to school. Oftentimes, we are waiting on God, but God is patiently waiting on us. So, do not get stuck in the tube of life any longer or delay your Purpose or Destiny. Do It Now!

***Philippians* 3:14** - *"I press on toward the goal to win the prize for which God has called me heavenward in Christ Jesus."*

> *"Don't get stuck; move quickly."*

Chapter Six

"Don't Put Me In A Box"

Even though Mary never had a child, and was a virgin; God did not put her in a box. His plan was to use someone different, someone that was innocent to carry the Messiah. Mary was young, holy and pure.

When people don't know or understand what God is doing in your life, because you are different and unique or simply because they think you don't fit the pattern for their circle, they will oftentimes; try to put you in a box. God doesn't need anyone's permission, before He chooses and equips whom He desires to use for His Purpose. I can see why God chose Mary; she did not fit into anyone's box and was the least likely to become pregnant.

One year, I was asked to speak at a Graduation for the Greater Miami Service Corp., a program that helped me when I dropped out of school; I humbly accepted the invitation and spoke at the graduation. This was an awesome opportunity to not only give back (pay it forward), but to encourage the graduates that they were in a position to do anything they put their mind to. I also shared that when I started the program two of my friends who started with me, dropped out and I kept going. Point to note: *"everyone that starts with you may not always finish with you."*

After the program, a young man from the audience walked over to me and congratulated me on my speech based on what I shared with them. He said, "listening to you speak, made me realize that *there is more to you than meets the eye.*" At that moment, I realized some people will judge you by your outward appearance not knowing what you are carrying on the inside.

Never let anyone put you in a box. There are people who looked at my outward appearance (my size and quiet spirit), the choices I made in life whether good or bad, and formed an opinion that I wasn't capable to fulfill my Purpose and Destiny. People will often categorize you by what you drive, where you live, how you look or even who you know.

They want you to be conformed into who they want or think you should be. Some people didn't want me to grow or move forward; because they couldn't see the bigger picture. They will even try to put you in a box to make themselves feel better about their own shortcomings and inabilities by using your past experiences to hold you back. Never hold yourself back because of people's opinion or perception of you. When God is ready to promote you to a new level, He will begin to nudge you in many different ways.

Remember to never lower your standard or abort your dreams and visions in order to fit in. Some people will only love you if you fit into their box. Always, be true to yourself and who God called you to be and don't be afraid to say No! I remember sharing my vision with someone and they told me that I wouldn't be able to do it, but then they turned around and asked me to help them reach their vision. In other words, lay my dreams down and work on theirs. See what I mean? Don't allow people to tell you who you are, instead, tell them who you are and whom God created you to be.

Ask yourself are you being boxed in? If so don't be afraid to disappoint; Break out of the Box.

> *"Never let anyone put you in a box.*
> *Don't be afraid to say No!"*

Chapter Seven

"Identify What You Are Carrying"

In the middle of a woman's pregnancy about 16-20 weeks, most are usually very excited to find out what 'sex' the baby will be; boy or girl.

For instance, when a woman goes to the doctor, she's usually surrounded by other women in the waiting room that are also pregnant. They will begin to converse with each other because of commonality i.e. how many weeks; what is the due date; is this baby number one; if it isn't, what number is this; how many siblings, girls vs. boys.

A small, but intimate room usually occupied with complete strangers, filled with chitter-chatter and excitement because Purpose is at

Identify What You Are Carrying

hand. Some may even exchange stories of their impending baby shower (if it hadn't already happened). Sharing, what a delight it is to go shopping to purchase all the necessary things for their anticipated bundle of joy.

I can remember how happy I was to watch the ultrasound, listen to the heart beat and finally to find out what I was carrying. Back then, it was really a *'faith'* viewing, as ultra sounds were not as sophisticated as they are today—3D views. The ultra sound was my proof that something was on the inside of me whether it was a boy, a girl or twins. The pure joy of simple knowing I was Pregnant with Purpose.

So, as it was with Mary and Elizabeth, both women were Pregnant with Purpose. Elizabeth was pregnant with *John the Baptist*; who was to prepare the way for the Messiah—Jesus and Mary, was pregnant with the Messiah!

Once you identify what you are carrying, whenever you are around others that are also Pregnant with Purpose, your baby will leap within your womb and you will be able to connect in *supernatural* ways.

When the Holy Spirit told me that I would write a book, He also told me, as a matter of fact; I will write several books. At that point, I identified that there was an author on the inside. Well, about six months later, I started looking on the internet for ghost writers, and later that same day that I began my search, I went to a one-night *Prophetic Activation* conference hosted by a well-known Apostle out of Chicago.

At a point in the conference, the Apostle instructed us to partner with someone that we didn't know in order to pray, and prophetically release to each other what we heard in our spirit.

I partnered with a young lady whom by the end of the night, we had discovered that our connection was a divine appointment, as our babies were leaping on the inside while we spoke to each other. After she prayed for me, the word she released was *"finish the book."* She then gave me her business card and, not only was she an author, but she was an editor, and a literary scribe or ghost writer. She also blessed me with a signed copy of her book and our divine friendship and journey began. And just

Identify What You Are Carrying

like God told Elizabeth that *John the Baptist* was predestined to prepare the way for Jesus; He told me that *"this lady was the one to prepare the way for my first book to come forth."* And that my fellow readers, was a *Supernatural Divine Connection*.

Additionally, my parent's absence from an early age in my life, created within me a passion to work with young adult women. This desire to give back and help them, led me to identify that there's an organization within waiting to be birthed which would allow me to fulfill my passion. Ask yourself what is your passion?

In summary, when you discover who you are in Him, it's not enough just to know that you are pregnant, you must also identify what you are pregnant with. Because once you have discovered your purpose, your desire and appetite will change and, not only will you want to be around people that have also discovered their purpose, but those that are literally Walking in It. Suddenly, your circle will begin to change; most likely it will decrease. You will only desire or crave to be around other destiny walkers; those Pregnant with Purpose.

You will also begin to connect with people that will want to help you to move forward. And believe it or not, your once decreasing circle will *supernaturally* begin to increase, but with quality people whom were sent divinely by the Father to connect to the destiny, vision, purpose and dreams within each of you.

> "When you are Walking in Purpose, God will supernaturally connect you with other Destiny Walkers."

Part II

2nd

TRIMESTER

Chapter Eight

"Rejection Will Not Stop Me"

When I realized I was Pregnant with Purpose, expectation and excitement filled my soul and I wanted everyone around me to share in and feel the same excitement and accept me for what I was carrying. But as a matter of fact, I learned quickly and the hard way, that my excitement was just that; my excitement. Unfortunately, we live in a cruel world where one-day people will love you and the next day, they are so ready to stone you. WOW, what an eye-opener that was.

People will begin speaking against your dreams and vision, they will question your purpose and what you are carrying and reject who you are. Oftentimes, when you are chosen and begin walking out your Purpose and

Rejection Will Not Stop Me

Destiny, people will reject you. Sadly, it's usually those closest to you, like family and friends.

I had to learn quickly to guard my heart. It doesn't matter how many people you may have helped and encouraged along the way, don't expect the same from everyone. Rejection may come simply because you are headed in a different direction. In other words, *"who do you think you are?"* The phone calls, text messages, and friendly visits may decrease or cease all together. When this happens, do not let rejection set in; remember to guard your heart. This, however, will be a sure indication that it's time to focus and draw nearer to God so you can hear Him clearly.

We must separate ourselves from all distractions and people whose time in our lifecycle may have expired. Don't despair, however, know that this is a realignment of sorts; a shift. You will begin to encounter divine connections and open doors through others that have been preselected for the journey that you are on.

Again, I say, guard your heart because it can be quite disappointing and painful. Especially when family members and close friends whom you thought would be with you through thick and thin, have suddenly, walked away. But take heed, God knows the plans He has for you:

Jeremiah 29:11 *"For I know the plans I have for you, declares the LORD, plans to prosper you and not to harm you, plans to give you hope and a future."*

So, be ready for doors to be closed that were once open. This doesn't mean give up, no, just move quickly to the next door. If you are anything like me, then expect to be hurt, you may cry and even question yourself, but be confident of this one thing that the ones who rejected you didn't know who you were and what you were carrying. I would venture to say that once the word was out that Mary was chosen out of all the other women, she began to experience rejection. *"Why would God choose her; what makes her better than any of us; she's carrying the Messiah?"*

Regardless of what people said about Mary or who rejected her; she was carrying Purpose and she didn't allow bitterness or offense to creep in. The same goes for you and I. People will reject you simply because you stepped out of your comfort zone to pursue your Purpose.

Rejection Will Not Stop Me

It's not for them to understand what God is doing in this season of your life. So, diligently guard your heart against all bitterness or offense.

Then, there are those whom will reject you just because you have stepped out and are now operating from another level which they have yet to reach. But, God in His immeasurable wisdom, will always have an answer ready and waiting for your rejection. God doesn't want us to depend on people, our job, our religious duties or our bank accounts. The Bible says *"the steps of a good man or woman are Ordered by Him."*

Don't allow rejection to stop you. God desires for you to follow the steps He has already mapped out for you.

> *"Don't allow Rejection to stop you; keep moving towards the Plan God has for you."*

Chapter Nine

"Move Past Intimidation"

Oftentimes, when a woman reaches the second trimester in her pregnancy, she enters the *uncomfortable zone*. This is the zone where the baby has gotten bigger. She can no longer see her swollen feet, her stomach has expanded, she's experiencing shortness of breath and every five (5) minutes or so, she has to use the bathroom. But the good thing is, she has one trimester remaining to be in this condition before delivery.

As a woman moves forward through each trimester, intimidation may try to set-in through people, places or things. Sometimes, when we walk in unfamiliar places, it will cause intimidation to creep in because we get too comfortable or complacent with where we are.

When what's on the inside of you moves you forward in a new direction, do not let people intimidate you or tell you differently. They will try to tell you that you are going in the wrong direction, and you are trying to do the impossible. As long as you are confident that you know and heard the Voice of God; move Forward and Move Past Intimidation!

There may be times when you find yourself in situations with other people that may know more than you, have more degrees than you, don't be intimidated. God will always equip those whom He calls. And if He has called you to give birth to what's on the inside of you then it's settled; you Will Deliver.

Jeremiah 1:8: *"Do not be afraid of their faces, For I am with you to deliver you," says the Lord."*

> *"Learn to stay focused and move past intimidation."*

Chapter Ten

"Don't Be Distracted By The Noise"

Distraction can be loud noises disguised as relationships, people with bad motives, unexpected events, a bad doctor's report, suddenly fired from your job, car-repossessed, spouse acting up, children rebelling, etc. and all for one reason, to take your focus off of your Purpose and your Destiny.

Every time distraction shows up, there's a sound attached to it, and when it does, how do we usually respond? We tend to stop and turn from our purpose and turn and focus on the noise. The intention of the noise is to derail us from our purpose.

Don't Be Distracted By The Noise

I can remember my second trimester of being Pregnant with Purpose, I began turning toward the noise that was coming from wrong friendships, relationships, family and just people in general; I was distracted by the noise of what people were doing around me.

In a previous Chapter, I spoke about how God had moved me from one place to another because I was focused on what others were doing, getting promoted and being pushed forward spiritually or naturally, I allowed distractions to blur my vision.

People close to me were being ordained in ministry, and I felt had I stayed, I too would have been ordained and promoted to the next level in ministry. After all, I was a Youth leader, I was teaching Sunday school, serving on the Missionary board, serving on the Finance committee and I was in the process of being added to the Church's board.

However, prior to their elevation, along came God, and pulled me out of my old familiar place; my comfort zone. I realized after, that if God had not moved me when He did, and had I not obeyed, the distraction of my loud thoughts of *"what about me,"* would have consumed me. I had to listen to God because I would have been out of position, out of the Will of God for my life, and I would have been distracted from my Purpose.

Positioned for Purpose, the battle of the mind ensued, as if having a tug of war with myself. Even though I was moving towards my destiny and who God called me to be, I was always second guessing myself because I was scared and complacent. I had to pull down the chain and break it in order to stay the course and continue to move towards my destiny. Oftentimes, I got distracted by dating the wrong person and ended up taking my eyes off my Purpose; focusing more on the person.

We must make sure that during our season of being Pregnant with Purpose, our relationships and friendships are ordained, if not, we must remove them or remove ourselves from them. Right relationships and friendships will not be a distraction to your purpose instead, they will push you towards your expected end.

The noise of Social Media is another big distraction. We are so focused on looking, liking and sharing what our peers, family, friends, strangers, and celebrities are posting that we lose valuable time being distracted. Social Media outlets are paid $billions of dollars each year to distract us from our Purpose. Instead, let's focus on using Social Media as a tool, a platform to promote our entrepreneurial dreams, visions, ideas, and talents.

When I started writing this book, I was distracted by the fact that so many people had already written books on the same topic; however, the Holy Spirit let me know that even though others wrote on the same topic, each of us have been given a measure of strategy for our personal journey into purpose. Though we have similar assignments, gifts and callings, know that no two will ever be the same. God will anoint you to carry out your purpose differently. Each individual is authentically designed to fulfill their preordained purpose; though Mary was chosen to carry the Messiah, there were many other women in the Bible whom were also Pregnant with Purpose.

I hope after reading this Chapter, you were able to identify distractions in your own life, if so, remove them NOW. Keep God first and remain in His Presence so you will be able to stay focused on what He has placed on the inside.

Remember, distractions will always surface when you are positioned to move forward to the next level. So, get rid of the noisy people and distractions and go forth towards your Purpose.

Proverbs 4:25 – *"Look straight ahead, and fix your eyes on what lies before you."*

> *"Never let people, places or things distract you from your Purpose."*

Part III

3rd

TRIMESTER

Chapter Eleven

"Do Not Move Before Time"

An estimated one in every ten infants born in the United States are premature or preemies.[4] A premature birth is a baby born before its completed 37 weeks of pregnancy. A full-term pregnancy is 40 weeks. Important growth and development happen throughout pregnancy – especially in the final months and weeks. Because they are born too early, preemies weigh much less than full term babies. They may have health problems because their organs did not have enough time to develop, such as breathing problems, feeding difficulties, cerebral palsy, developmental delay, vision problems, hearing

---

[4] https://www.cdc.gov.

problems; to name a few. Preemies may need special medical care in a neonatal care unit or NICU where they will stay until their system can function on its own.

When moving forward toward our Purpose and Destiny, we get so excited because we are close to giving birth. We want to share with the world that our purpose is at hand. We want everyone to know that we are Pregnant with Purpose; we begin opening up and sharing our dreams, visions and purpose in order to connect with different people.

It is vital to move in God's timing concerning our Purpose and Destiny. We do not want to move or make any decisions before time because we cannot afford to give birth to our Purpose prematurely. I shared with one of my close friends about writing this book, she asked me, *"what is your target date to finish your book?"* When I told her my target date, and everything I desired to do; she didn't understand. Instead, she had more questions: *"why did you pick that month to release your book;*

when will you have everything finished; why did you wait so long—you should have been finished with your book, and you don't have to do everything all at once."

Though she meant well, what she didn't understand was that the purpose of my book had to be fully developed. I had to feed my purpose, study my purpose, become comfortable in my purpose. I had to cultivate my purpose so that what I was about to birth wouldn't have birth defects. I had to make sure the right people were around me, and make the necessary preparations so as not to have a premature baby. That's why it was so important for me to invest in a coach.

God told me that my target date to let the world know would be January 2018, even though the book was completed in late 2017. He was letting me know, I was about to leave the old and walk into the new; God is always doing and speaking something new. I was leaving the old year and walking into a New Year; do not be in a hurry to give birth, and move out of God's appointed time before your Purpose is fully matured and developed. A pregnant woman has to make sure she is taking all her vitamins, eating the right food for proper nutrition, getting the necessary rest and removing anything that would harm her pregnancy, in order for her to give birth to a fully developed baby or God's Promise. You too need to take the necessary steps by feeding your purpose, acquiring the right equipment, attending school if necessary, and investing in a coach or a mentor. This will avoid moving before time and giving birth to a premature purpose.

> *"Make sure your Purpose is fully developed and matured before giving birth."*

Chapter Twelve

"Release the Hurt"

Throughout my pregnancy, I went through a lot of hurt and disappointment from people I thought had my back; people whom I believed I could trust and confide in. But instead, all the gossiping and backbiting drove me *figuratively*, into a cave for shelter; I didn't want to be bothered by or with anyone.

Have you ever been hurt by a person or persons in the name of *'I did it for you …?'* Well, if you haven't, just continue living. Allow me to be transparent for a moment and tell you first hand; the *pain of betrayal*, can be *crippling*. I wouldn't wish that suffering on my worst enemy. Sometimes in life, certain circumstances, situations and bad decisions we may make, whether it be spiritual or in the natural, oftentimes bring out the worst in people who believes whole heartedly, that it's their *calling*, their God given duty to give you their judgmental opinions or position themselves as the Voice of I AM in your life.

Sadly, I had no choice, but to cut people from the different rows in my life and some who didn't even have a row to speak of. Some of these people I dearly loved, but couldn't trust if I was to survive and give birth to a new life. I was hearing that people were sending word curses my way, stating I would never make it. However, their perception of me was that I was *a commoner*, but on the contrary, there was nothing *common* about me. Though the enemy had an *assassin-hit* out on my life, God's hand was on me from childhood; which qualified me to be supernaturally *uncommon—out of the ordinary, unusual, rare, exceptional*.

The terror onslaught started from a child and transitioned into relationships; causing pain and hurt even in the religious arena. I encountered witches, warlocks and wizards that wanted to control and hurt me, but that which was placed inside me from my mother's womb, never allowed me to give up and cave in.

Fast forward…. I had to move past all of the past hurt and pain, I had to Forgive; I had to release ALL Unforgiveness. Forgiveness is hard; but mandatory. Once I let go of **ALL** the past hurt, bitterness and the offense, the unnecessary weight was released and my labor pains kicked in. In order to give birth to Purpose, we must first let go of all the unnecessary weight; that weight for me was Unforgiveness. Ponder for a moment and ask the Holy Spirit to reveal to you any Unforgiveness you may have in your heart, so that whatever is weighing you down can be released. If you do not let Unforgiveness go, it will mess up your Purpose. Do it now, and be FREE!

Once I let it go, I realized the negative impact the hurt and pain was having on my character and how it was stealing my Purpose. On the outside, I appeared to be whole, but on the inside, I was messed up from past hurt and pain. However, these experiences were teaching me how not to treat people; teaching me how to release my baggage in order to walk out and into my Purpose. Because I Trusted God during my process (we each have a personalized process), I was able to give birth to my Purpose, filled with Life and it wasn't one day late.

One of the unfortunate things about giving birth to a still born in the natural is that your body will still experience the birthing process, i.e. contractions, labor pains, and the end result will always be grief and no life. However, when your Purpose is still born, it's usually because you didn't complete the process and you likely gave up and caved in; but be Encouraged!

The mere fact that you are reading this book, means the Holy Spirit has bestowed His Favor, Grace and Mercy upon you. You should now have a better understanding of the Power of Forgiveness and the importance of being delivered from people that could get in the way and block your Purpose. As for me, at that juncture, learning to forgive and releasing the hurt was the best thing that happened to me. God delivered me from my Pain into my Purpose and lovingly, guided me Forward, closer to my Destiny.

When we have failed to give birth to Purpose, fear not, because all have not been lost, as God will give you a new "due season" and you will begin to develop again, and your tailor-made process will continue until you have succeeded. In order to make sure our Purpose is alive and well, we must allow God to deliver us from people.

> *"Release the hurt, bitterness and unforgiveness and Push past the Pain."*

Chapter Thirteen

"It's Time To Deliver"

You can now assume the posture to give birth and position those whom will be in the delivery room with you. So, gird up your loins and strap your legs in and get ready to push. Push what God has prewired you with because your Purpose has fully matured and developed. You now have the platform, attitude, and the right mindset to overcome; you can now sit at the table with kings, queens and priests; you can now walk with your head held high; you now have all the confidence needed; you can now be seated at boardroom tables; you can now be in the company of your haters and enemies and you won't be affected because you can now walk into rooms and Shift the Atmosphere.

You experienced the labor pains and dominated the process. Now you can own your Purpose and no one can change your mind.

DELIVER YOUR BABY!!!!!!

PRAYER

Father God, in the Name of Jesus we lift up to you, each person that is reading this book, stir up what is on the inside of them. Give them the boldness and clarity on how to bring their purpose forward. Begin to surround them with the right people that will push them forward. Heavenly Father, remove anything that will try to block, delay or forfeit their purpose. I decree and declare creative ideas, business plans, inventions, influence, divine connections, and finances to birth out their purpose. Lord, we thank you for the process of identifying when we become pregnant, the 1st trimester, the 2nd trimester, and the 3rd trimester in order to give birth to our destiny, dreams, goals, and purpose. In Jesus Name we pray, AMEN.

www.ingramcontent.com/pod-product-compliance
Lightning Source LLC
Chambersburg PA
CBHW051702090426
42736CB00013B/2506